For our family, friends, and followers joining this journey one step at a time. —Kentee P.

For Winston, Check and all my fostered friends. —Bonnie K.

Text and Illustration Copyright © 2025 by Bonnie Kelso
Text Copyright © 2025 by Kentee Pasek

All rights reserved. No part of this book may be reproduced in any manner or transmitted in any form without the express written consent of the publisher, except in the case of brief excerpts in critical reviews and articles. For permission inquiries, please contact info@gnomeroadpublishing.com.

GNOME ROAD PUBLISHING
Louisville, KY, USA
www.gnomeroadpublishing.com
Logo designs by Wendy Leach, Copyright © 2025 by Gnome Road Publishing
Book design by Bonnie Kelso.

Library of Congress Control Number: 2024948560
LC record available at: https://lccn.loc.gov/2024948560

978-1-957655-48-2 (trade) | 978-1-957655-50-5 (ebook)

Summary: The story of how the three-legged internet sensation taught himself to walk upright like a human after an accident, sharing a message of resilience, joy, and how to take challenging situations "one Dexter-step at a time."

Illustrations were rendered digitally.
The text of this book is set in Capitolina, Peachy Keen, and Nudgewink Pro fonts.

First Edition
10 9 8 7 6 5 4 3 2 1
Manufactured in China

DEXTER
The Stand Up Dog

Written by
Bonnie Kelso
Kentee Pasek

Illustrated by
Bonnie Kelso

Dexter took his first puppy steps
on a crisp, clear Colorado spring day.
He soon found his forever home.

One step.   **Two steps…**

Three! Dexter found his family!

Dexter loved to run! But sometimes . . .

. . . he ran too fast.

Dexter was a lot like other puppies.
Tasty treats warmed his tummy.

Belly rubs made him wiggle-waggle.

He had a favorite ball!

One day, before anyone could stop him,
Dexter slipped out the front door,

bounded down the steps,
over the fence, and . . .

Dexter was hurt! Mom and Dad rushed him to the hospital.

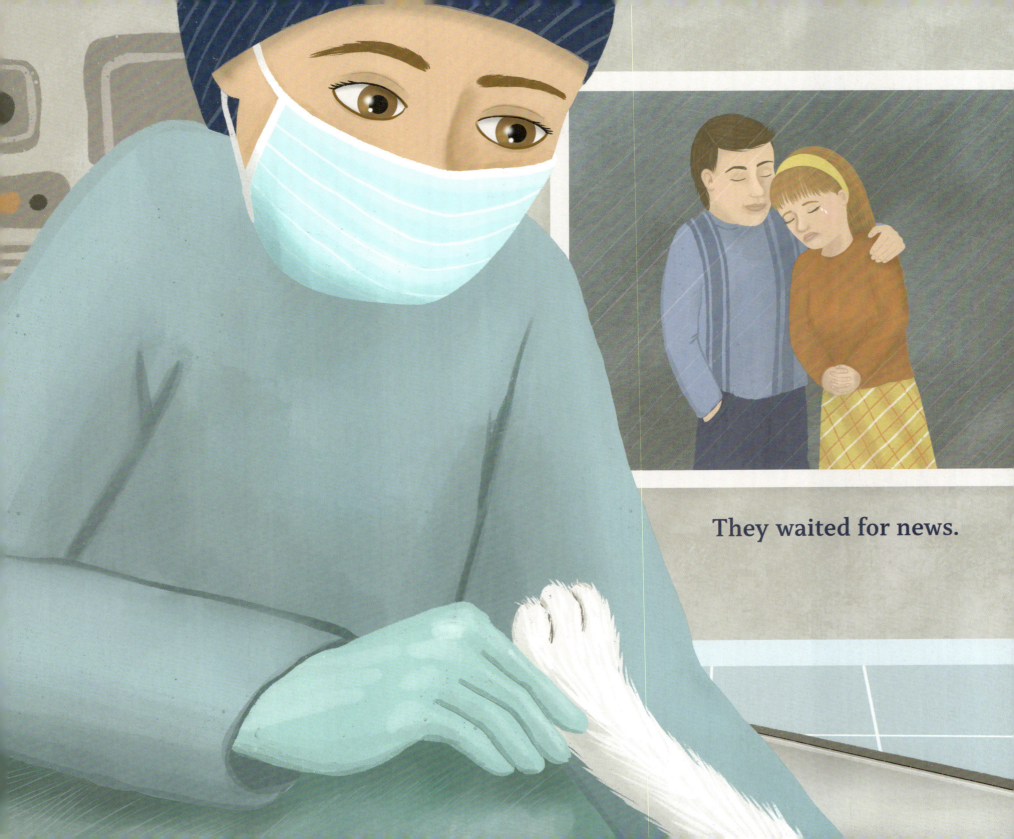

They waited for news.

After a long sleep, Dexter woke up. Sore and nervous, he thought of his family to feel better.

Finally, after several days,
Dexter's family could take him home.

"Awww, his tail is wagging."

"We missed you, Dexter!"

He was happy to be together again.

At first, Dexter was very confused.
One leg was missing and one leg
didn't work very well.

Even so, Dexter was determined
to zoom around again.

Dexter's family knew how much he loved to go fast, so they gave him a race car.

It was okay,

but he wanted to go faster.

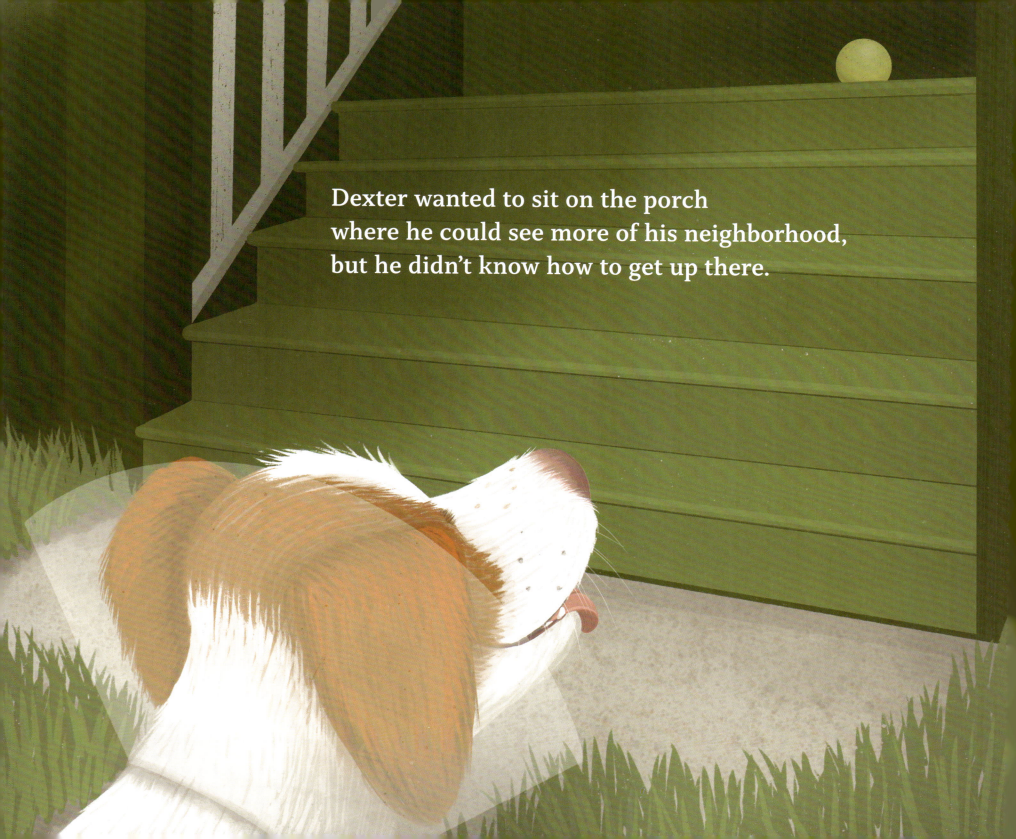

Dexter wanted to sit on the porch where he could see more of his neighborhood, but he didn't know how to get up there.

So, he balanced on his two hind legs.
They shook and wobbled.
He stood, but only for one second.

Dexter was determined.

He tried again.

Three steps . . .

Two steps.

One step.

Dexter did it!

The more Dexter practiced, the better he got, and soon he was walking, skipping, and hopping on two legs.

It was fun being tall.
Dexter could see everything.

When he walked through town,
he saw food on tables, goodies inside bags,
and lots of smiling faces.

But then, everything changed again. To be safe, people had to stay home.

Seeing videos of Dexter walking made them feel good while they were locked down. That's when Dexter, the stand up dog, became an internet sensation!

The more people learned what Dexter could do, the more they wanted to meet him.

Dexter's joy and positivity spread

like sunshine over everyone he met.

Each day became a new adventure for Dexter and his family. They were on TV, met celebrities, and visited children all over the country.

Dexter discovered something new, too!

He learned that the
best part about traveling
is coming home again . . .

and that any challenge
can be overcome,
one Dexter-step at a time.

Kentee Pasek became a full-time content creator in June 2020. She holds a degree in Recreation Administration and Fine Art from the University of Northern Colorado. A lifelong love of animals and fascination with photography and video production propelled her into social media. The story of her beloved upright-walking dog Dexter became her sole focus on many different platforms online. Kentee and her family live in Ouray, Colorado, returning to her hometown after her husband retired from the Coast Guard. The backdrop of this stunning mountain town and the unique upright walking ability of Dexter turned this Brittany Spaniel dog into an inspirational star. To learn more about this journey visit www.dexterdogouray.com

Bonnie Kelso studied art at the Rhode Island School of Design where she met the first dog she ever fell in love with—a boxer named Check. Now she lives in Las Vegas with her family, a tortoiseshell cat named Frida, and a Boston Terrier named Winston. She often volunteers as a foster parent for a local dog rescue group. Dogs keep her happy (and her feet warm) while she writes and illustrates books for children. To learn more about Bonnie and her work, visit www.BonnieKelso.com.

Scan to learn more about Dexter.

Scan to learn more about Gnome Road Publishing.